CARRIE KIPLING
1862-1939

First published in 2001 by
Short Books
15 Highbury Terrace
London N5 1UP

A CIP catalogue record for this book
is available from the British Library.

ISBN 0 571 20835 5

Printed in Great Britain by
Bookmarque Ltd, Croydon, Surrey

THE HATED WIFE

CARRIE KIPLING
1862-1939

ADAM NICOLSON

✳ SHORT BOOKS

Carrie

For Sarah, the beloved wife

WHEN RUDYARD KIPLING first met her, Carrie Balestier wore her hair pulled tightly back from her forehead, with a central parting, and the thick bulk of a brown plait pinned with combs in a knot. It was a style which exposed an almost masculine face: straight, black eyebrows; inquiring, interrogative eyes; a nose not exactly aquiline but too long for conventional beauty; strong teeth (unlike her husband's which were rotten in his twenties) and a prominent jaw. Hers was a face that could take on the world. When Rudyard Kipling's father first saw her, inspecting her, anxiously looking at the American who, it was being said, would take over his son's life, all he saw in her was 'a good man spoiled'.

As the years passed and the sequence of catastrophes began to tell, her full lips became thinner, the mouth itself began to turn down, and her chin and jaw thickened. Her body became a barograph of her tragedy, and a life that had begun so forthrightly turned into a retreat and a defeat. Her increasing bulk enclosed and protected an ever more shattered core.

Caroline Balestier was 26 when she arrived in England in 1889. She approached the world with an American certainty and would never have been content, as late Victorian London might have preferred, to submit to the decorative role the English still required of their women. Her background would not have allowed her that sort of passivity. The Balestiers had emerged from several generations of raw, moneymaking ventures in the New World. The beginnings of their fortune had been made on slave-worked sugar plantations in Martinique. There were certainly French and Spanish elements in their ancestry. Their riches had been boosted by property deals in the wilds of Chicago in the 1830s, and then swelled further when Carrie's grandfather moved to the abundant pickings of New York. Ball-breaking, unsentimental frontier entrepreneurship was embedded in the family culture. It was married to another strain. Carrie's grandmother was a Wolcott, a member of the deepest, most East Coast, New England, Puritan establishment. She counted governors of Connecticut and Paul Revere among her treasured ancestors. Through her, patrician, gubernatorial, Wasp assumptions of a right to significance had been grafted on to the Balestier vigour.

In Carrie's father, this potent mix went awry. Henry Balestier's career as a lawyer did not thrive. He was a dreamer, rather than a businessman, with a whimsical and eccentric sense of humour. He drifted into insurance broking, an occupation he did not enjoy, and which was not helped by his own sickliness. He died after 10 years of marriage, having been first a bad father to his children and then an absent one. His wife Anna, the daughter of a lawyer herself, effectively brought up the children alone.

Carrie was eight when her father died, and soon afterwards her mother took her and her three siblings from the Balestier house in New York City to her father's house, in the small town of Rochester, in upstate New York. The arrival of the unconventional Balestiers was not exactly what the citizens of Rochester wanted. They brought their chaos with them, and the Balestier house, on Lexington Avenue, was famous for its strangeness. 'There is no doubt,' one of their neighbours remembered, 'that all the Balestiers had a share of the brilliancy... With it went strong personalities, independence of thought, and impatience with conventionalities – in fact, all the qualities best calculated to shock and surprise well-conducted mediocrity.'

Already by her teens, Carrie was seen as headstrong, unattractively interested in art and poetry, prepared to stand outside the norm. She was 'fond of extremes in dress, wearing the largest and loudest checks, when checks were in fashion, and outraging convention in the matter of color and size of hats and ties'. She had inherited her father's romantic disengagement, with 'the air of habitually living in a world apart from those around her. She was a hero-worshipper, her mind at that time being filled with the desire to visit far countries and live a life of activity which was far from being the "ladylike" ideal for the feminine sex in that day.'

The Balestiers were, above all, a family of individuals. Of Carrie's three siblings, Josephine, the youngest, was the weakest. The only pretty one in the family, she was a 'delicate' child, treated more or less as an invalid. Carrie throughout her life looked down on her as the little girl, and Josephine would refer to herself as 'little Miss J'. When they were both in their sixties, Carrie could still tick her off for not replying to letters. Beatty, the younger of the two brothers, was a naughty boy, and consistently indulged. He grew up to be a drunk, wisecracking ne'er-do-well, drawing more on the Balestier than the Wolcott inheritance, and was for Carrie a source of irritation, and often loathing. She dismissed him either as a boor or a sponge. The elder brother, Wolcott, was the hero of the family. Brilliant, if a little shambolic, here was the heir to the full Balestier-Wolcott inheritance. For a while he was a student at Cornell but he couldn't make it stick. On two occasions he then tried an adventurous life in the wild American West, where Carrie accompanied him, but that didn't work either. He then edited a low-brow weekly gossip-sheet called *Tid-Bits* in New York. Not exactly handsome, cursed with the Balestier nose and a little degenerate about the eyes, he was nevertheless charming, flirtatious, demanding and, in the way he dealt with family, friends and clients, powerful. Those who knew him became wary of his egotism. As one of them, the American artist Charles Bacon, wrote: 'Wolcott Balestier is a good friend but allows *no one* to stand in the way of his success. He is a Czar in his family. No one apparently expects that anyone can suit him or get on with him in business because of his electrical ways and dictatorship.'

Wolcott was in many ways the man Carrie might have been. They shared most of their characteristics: pride, pugnaciousness, contempt for fools, a habit of direction and control. In another age, she might have had a career in business or the law. But those possibilities would never have occurred to her. She loved her brother and was happy to be his helpmate. If the ecology of all families divides, in the end, into winners and losers, Carrie saw herself and Wolcott as the winning team, Beatty and Josephine as the no-hopers, to be patronised, helped and pitied.

It was in Wolcott's wake that Carrie first came to England in June 1889. He had been taken on as a London agent by John Lovell, an American publisher, on whose magazine he had been working. The situation over copyright for European authors in the United States was in a state of chaos. Piracy was rife. Balestier was sent to London in December 1888 to offer English authors the prospect of secure American sales, an American income from simultaneous publication on both sides of the Atlantic and syndication rights. His charm, energy and the widening prospect he presented of a dollar-strewn continent could not fail to appeal. Literary London was ripe for the picking. The world of English letters was a combination of lush aestheticism and a new hunger for the market. The word 'bestseller' had just been coined. The possibility of global sales for successfully marketed authors had for the first time been recognised. It was just the environment in which the Balestiers could thrive.

With this triumph in prospect, Carrie came to keep house for Wolcott in Neville Terrace in Kensington; in effect to act as hostess, to create a salon around him in which the boundaries of business and friendship could be seductively elided.

It was a role for which she was entirely suited. She was not frightened by the reputations of the men Wolcott set out to woo. She thought highly of herself and rated her ability to manipulate others. And there was a third quality: a belief that as a woman she was there to serve. Wolcott, just a year older than her, was to be looked after. He was the great and admirable man. She was to allow him to flower.

'Please don't forget', she wrote to her younger sister Josephine when Josephine raised the possibility of a literary career, 'that being a plain woman who does a woman's work is not a career to turn away from. It does not seem to have the rewards that some others have but it must have its secret. For myself, I do not care for literary women, not those that I know, and as you know them too, it will be easier to plan yourself differently.'

Carrie, voluble letter writer as she was, was never to be a literary rival to her brother or her husband. That was not a role she ever wanted or could have fulfilled.

A valuable throng of late Victorian figures was corralled through the Balestier house in Kensington and the office in Dean's Yard in Westminster: Edmund Gosse and his wife Nellie ('Dear old NG', as Carrie refers to her), the Whistlers, the painter Lawrence Alma-Tadema, Ouida, Henry James, Bram Stoker, the young publisher William Heinemann, who became Wolcott's partner in a European publishing venture, Kate Greenaway, Austin Dobson, George Meredith, Mrs Thomas Hardy, Mrs Humphry Ward: all could be led to market.

Carrie set out her stall. 'What I want to do is to be most discrete,' she wrote, misspelling as she would for the rest of her life, to Josephine, 'and not get into the vulgar London way of saying so-and-so is to be at my afternoon, do come, but to get them so well started from the word go that if anyone stays away they will hear directly what they have missed.'

All of the Balestiers were regularly coming and going across the Atlantic. In the autumn of 1890, their brother Beatty and his new wife Mai, a local Vermont girl, visited London. Carrie, anxious at the gaffes these potentially embarrassing relations might make, had a plan, as she described to Josephine: 'I have a chest of drawers in the corner. I would try the tea there and if Mai is here have her pour it and stay in that corner. I am thinking of what flowers to have and shall have all the little tables so people can put their cups on them. I think I must have a choice collection of Fuller candy. There are two stumbling blocks after people have fallen over Mrs Whistler and her most frightful sister. There is Madame Gosse and Madame Harland. But we will see. We have discovered to our satisfaction that we can get Henry James when we really want him and so we are going to indulge him and let him stay away except when he is really needed to impress.'

Naive as this was, Carrie clearly had little idea of the impression she was making. Henry James, the king of transatlantic culture and connoisseur of the 'American girl', might have been Carrie's champion. In many ways she represented the type he had made famous: all the vigour of America set against the crumbly derelictions of Europe; new world courage against old world compromise. He might have loved her, but his attentions were directed instead towards her brother, who was cleverer and subtler than her, more able to conceal his ruthlessness. Brute toughness, which was always an element in Carrie, was anathema to James. And she was too mundane; too bound up in the facts and reality of daily existence. It was Wolcott's quivering, mercurial presence which drew him; his ability to achieve an almost instant, quasi-sexual intimacy. If Henry James was coming to Neville Terrace, it was not for Carrie's company. He admired her courage, but that was not enough. For James, the sister was 'a hard, devoted, capable little person'.

At first quite unacquainted with the Balestiers, Rudyard Kipling had come to London in September 1889. He was 24, world-famous, already published all over the English-speaking world, drawing vast royalty cheques from all corners of the empire, pirated and cheated by American publishers, the subject of an adulatory leader in *The Times*, compared with Dickens and Maupassant, described as 'the hope for English literature', applauded and doted on by the central figures in the English literary establishment.

Kipling rapidly came to despise the fawning old men, the lion-eating hostesses and the exhausted aesthetes of 1890s London. Party after party of overheated adulation left him disgusted and cynical: 'I kept thinking to

myself, "Unless it happened that I was the fashion for the moment, you'd let me die of want on your doorstep." '
After one cab ride with Sidney Colvin, the curator of prints and drawings at the British Museum and author of a late, lush biography of Keats, dripping with homoerotic longing, Kipling was merciless: 'The same is an all-fired prig of immense water and suffers from all the nervo-hysterical disease of the 19th century. He recounted all his symptoms and made me sick.'

The young genius newly arrived from India had deliberately avoided taking lodgings anywhere near the Kensington drawing-rooms of the literati, instead renting rooms in the narrow trench of Villiers Street next to Charing Cross station, from where he could watch and engage with the more common realities, 'the miles of seething vice thrust out upon the street', threading his way home late at night through the whores – the *papillons de nuit* – plying for trade in the gutters of the Strand.

His two rooms were decorated in a combination of the manly, the undergraduate and the exotic – a demonstration more of what he wanted to be than what he was. On the door he had pinned a notice – 'To publishers: a classic while you wait', while the rooms themselves were papered in green and gold, full of Persian rugs and ancient prayer carpets, with a tall Japanese screen on which skeletons danced across the lacquer. There were pictures of soldiers in India on the walls and a map of Afghanistan. A bundle of fishing rods stood in the corner and, above the fireplace, a little eccentrically for the middle of London, hung a new rifle with a loaded magazine.

In fact, the Kipling with whom Rider Haggard, Edmund Gosse, Henry James and half the editors of London were now so delighted was an emotional wreck. The knowing familiarity of his Indian tales, and the apparent intimacy of his knowledge of the soldier classes and the Indian slums, was an elaborate literary artefact set above a personality that was desperately insecure.

An emotional vacuum had dominated his childhood. When he was six, his adored mother and father had abandoned both him and his younger sister Trix in a boarding house in Southsea. They didn't see their parents again for six years. Trix later wrote, 'I think the real tragedy of our early days... sprang from our inability to understand why our parents had deserted us. We had had no preparations or explanation; it was like a double death, or rather like an avalanche that had swept away everything happy and familiar.'

This incomprehensible act of cruelty could never be forgotten. Life in the boarding house was bleak and mean. The young boy was accused by the landlady and her bullying son of cheating and forced to walk through the streets of Southsea with a placard on his back bearing the one word 'LIAR'. The untrustworthiness of human nature, the unreliability of those who say they love you, the threat of anarchic pain behind even the most secure-seeming institutions and arrangements: these were the attitudes that were to shape the man. 'When young lips', he wrote at the end of his life, 'have drunk deep of the bitter nature of Hate, Suspicion, and Despair, all the Love in the world will not wholly take away that knowledge.'

When, after six years, his mother finally came from India to see him in the Southsea boarding lodge, she arrived unannounced. Young Ruddy was in bed. As she bent down to kiss him, he raised his hand to ward off the blow he was expecting. The kiss that might also be a blow, the adored mother who could hurt him this deeply, the substitution of all the riches of India for the sterility of the south coast of England: is it any wonder that the child learned that distrust was the only reasonable attitude?

Kipling in his Villiers Street rooms was struggling with the turbulence of his own self: the febrile gaiety, the ambition and the sense of winning were combined with a feeling of irrelevance, of purposelessness, feeling himself pitted against a literary establishment he despised. He was prone to repeated breakdown from overwork and was tempted to withdraw from a world he wanted to own. He loved his father, a wise, stable figure, but was in many ways still his mother's son. More than anyone, Alice Kipling, who was herself a subtly dominant figure, was aware and protective of his fragilities.

Kipling and the Balestiers eventually met each other, probably in February or March 1890. It was not Carrie with whom Kipling fell in love but her brother Wolcott. Although it was never quite clear if Wolcott was homosexual, an almost sexual agitation was in the air around him. Old Edmund Gosse felt 'a thrill of attraction' for him, fluttering with excitement at his mixture of 'the suave Colonial French and the strained nervous New England blood'. A kind of fevered intimacy hung about Wolcott's male, literary and painterly circle. The wives, where there were any, were considered a little ridiculous and supernumerary.

Did Kipling and Wolcott become lovers? Some of Kipling's biographers have thought so, and the way in which, in his later life, Kipling wrote and spoke with such frantic loathing of homosexuality as a beastly and bestial business has been taken as a sign that they were. There were clearly feminine elements to them both. Wolcott would wear a lily in his lapel. In photographs Kipling's stance is always a little feminine, one knee half bent, chin raised in the way of short men making a claim on the world, but with a tension in him, as if his weight were resting on the balls of his feet, ready to leave. He was clearly in love with a certain kind of masculinity and was openly drawn to masculine women. Perhaps there might have been a flirtation between him and the universally alluring Wolcott. But as the Kiplings would later destroy as much written evidence of their past lives as they could get their hands on, the material no longer exists on which any judgment can be made. Wolcott and Kipling were close; that is all that can be said.

The friendship developed rapidly and within a few weeks 'the two young lions', as Josephine rather coyly described them, were staying up all night talking. They embarked on the writing of a novel together. Drunken dinners were held in Kipling's Villiers Street rooms. And from most of this Carrie was not excluded. She introduced Kipling to the delights of popcorn at his birthday party. (Or at least she tried to: the corn she had bought refused to pop.) She taught him how to type, close together over the keys of a machine which she had only recently mastered herself. Kipling began to keep some clothes in the Balestier office in Westminster. He demanded, so Carrie told her wide-eyed sister at home in Vermont, that a place should be set for him at every meal – lunch and dinner – whether he was expected or not.

He was an exciting presence in the Balestiers' lives, a famous writer but younger than them and with no respect for the world of literary grandee-dom they were all attempting to penetrate. Although Kipling was already bald, he was boyish in appearance and manner, talking nineteen to the dozen, irreverent, coarse, sitting with one leg over the arm of a chair, slovenly in his dress, wearing rough flannel shirts and jackets whose pockets were filled to bulging; and colluding with Wolcott and the girls against the ancient pomposities by whom they were surrounded.

'The Gosses are wildly jealous of our intimacy with Kipling,' Carrie wrote to her younger sister, 'though of course I never mention his comings and goings to them but he doesn't mind if I do and they hear as everyone always does and to see him here is enough for he acts as if he were familiar with it all and of course they have not the sense to know that he would do that anyway.'

Carrie's proprietorial air had begun to alarm those who were watching. 'That woman', Kipling's mother said on first setting eyes on her, 'is going to marry our Ruddy.'

Without Wolcott, it is unlikely that Kipling would have spent the time he did with the Balestiers. But he was promiscuous with his charm. He flirted as much with Josephine as he did with Carrie and Wolcott. If Rudyard was having a love affair, it was with the whole family. And he wooed them all. 'I find the young man the pleasantest article in London, he is so refreshingly unEnglish,' Carrie wrote back from one of her sallies. 'And for some unknown reason I have never had any shyness with him and can be myself when he is about because it is a nagging bother to be overwhelmed and unable to be oneself all the time.' By the beginning of 1891, Carrie was clearly in a position of great intimacy and influence with both her brother and Kipling. A decision made jointly by Wolcott and Carrie had persuaded Kipling that the book on which he was working, 'The Book of the Forty-Five Mornings', should be abandoned. 'I read them in proofs,' Carrie wrote to Josephine, now back in America, 'and agreed with Wolcott who made him stop them, that for the most part they were not the stuff that he ought to give the world now, they were the youngest thing he had by him and it was a shame to let them see daylight here.'

These signals were being read carefully by the Kipling family. Rudyard's mother, Alice, became anxious about the way Caroline Balestier was poring over her son, claiming him as her own. She must also have been worried about the friendship with Wolcott. Kipling was now working closely with him on the novel, and staying regularly with him in Wolcott's cottage on the Isle of Wight. Alice feared that her son might collapse. Certainly, there were signs of crisis in Kipling's body. He woke one morning to find his left eyelid dropped, his left side stiff and not under control and with cramp on the left side of his face. He had reached breaking-point.

There are one or two hints, although the whole question is surrounded by such secrecy that no one can be sure, that by the autumn of 1891 Kipling had become engaged to Carrie. If so, it would have been part of an habitual pattern. Since his teens, his life had been a lurching series of emotional muddles. Repeatedly, he had attached himself to older, stronger women and had then grown alarmed as they became attached to him. Twice already he had been engaged, or virtually engaged, to women whom he had then left for some other part of the globe. The year before he had even proposed, and been accepted by, another young American woman, Carrie Taylor, with whose older sibling, a married woman called Ted Hill, he had been distantly in love for years. The engagement had atrophied on Kipling's arrival in London. Two American Carries, both younger sisters of powerfully attractive figures, neither of whom was conventionally available to him (Wolcott a man, Ted Hill married): this alone is testimony to the precarious state of Kipling's emotions. Now again, just as he had with his previous fiancées, he decided that he had to 'get clean away and re-sort myself'. He set off on 8 August 'on a small expedition to the other end of the world'. He would visit his hero Robert Louis Stevenson in Samoa.

Soon after Kipling left, Wolcott went to Germany on a business trip to promote the European editions of the authors he represented. Carrie waited in London for her mother, Anna, and her sister, Josephine, and the three women then travelled together to Paris. It was a party out of a Henry James novel. Carrie could conduct her provincial relations around the glories of a Europe to which she now felt she had some claim. Life was as good as it had ever been. Wolcott's business was thriving. Everybody in London loved him. Carrie knew, it seems, that Kipling loved her. The future looked like a sequence of possibilities.

This Elysian picture then imploded. News reached Carrie and her family at the end of November that Wolcott had fallen ill in Germany and they felt they should go there to see him. They travelled by train to Dresden but only on arrival there realised how ill he was. His condition was horrifying: he was already infected with typhoid fever, although not yet unconscious. He asked Carrie to check some of the proofs of the novel he had been writing with Kipling and then send them to America. All of the Balestier women recognised that Wolcott's life was in danger and they attended to him as never before, plying him with port, beef tea and milk. The fever heightened and they bathed him three times a day, witnessing the shrinking away of his body to a skeleton. Finally he became delirious, veering wildly in his states of consciousness, babbling of his hopeless younger brother Beatty, and on 6 December he died.

The family was devastated. Anna Balestier had lost her husband after ten years of marriage and now she had lost her eldest child. Carrie had lost the man she loved. Wolcott had been the sun around which the Balestiers revolved. His death left them centreless and, in the terrifying zero-gravity of the aftermath, Carrie sent Kipling a telegram: 'WOLCOTT DEAD STOP COME BACK TO ME STOP.' He replied by wire, asking her to marry him.

The funeral was held in Dresden. William Heinemann, Wolcott's business partner, and Henry James came out to attend, but neither of them played any part in the arrangements. It was Carrie who was in control of events. James described to Gosse: 'poor little concentrated, passionate Carrie, remarkable in her force, acuteness, capacity, and courage – and in the intense – almost manly nature of her emotion. She is a worthy sister of poor dear, big-spirited, only-by-death-quenchable Wolcott.' The hard, capable little person had found her hour. She arranged for Wolcott's possessions in London to be hidden so that neither her mother nor Josephine, who was incapacitated with distress, would see them when they returned. Remarkably, she also instructed that his American newspaper subscriptions should now be sent to her under the name of 'Mrs Wolcott Balestier'. Was this a recognition, however subliminal, that she was now, in a strange sense, a widow?

Kipling returned from Bombay to London in ten days. Carrie, Josephine and their mother met him at Victoria station and he took out a special marriage licence the following day. The 'dreary little wedding', as Henry James described it, took place in the fog on 18 January 1892. Almost no one was there. Anna and Josephine Balestier and both of Kipling's parents were in bed with flu. The whole of London was down with it and the undertakers had run out of black horses. 'The dead had to be content with brown ones,' Kipling wrote in his autobiography. A lugubrious coterie of men – Henry James, Edmund Gosse and William Heinemann, who was late – attended the rapid, secretive, uncelebratory service. Kipling had been 'hurried into matrimony like a rabbit into its hole', Gosse told a friend in America. 'It is Caroline, of course, not pretty Josephine who is now "Mrs RK".' Henry James was no more enthusiastic: 'I don't in the least understand his marrying. It's a union of which I don't forecast the future though I gave her away at the altar.' Neither Kipling nor Carrie wanted anyone to know.

**

Wolcott would hang over the Kiplings' marriage like a ghost. His name could never be mentioned in their presence again. No photograph of him was ever to be found in their houses. Neither his name nor his existence appeared in Kipling's autobiography, written over four decades after Wolcott's death. In the thousands of letters and the daily diary which Carrie wrote between her marriage and Kipling's death, Wolcott is referred to perhaps four or five times. His life and his memory, central to their lives and marriage, had to be expunged.

The Kiplings' reaction to pain throughout their lives would always be the same: repression. Not that gloom hung over everything. Kipling would always be playful in adversity. The voyage they took across the Atlantic after the wedding, despite the ghosts and the presence of Anna and Josephine Balestier, was filled with gaiety and, apparently, almost Wagnerian lust:

> I was the Lord of the Inca Race, and she was the Queen of
> the Sea.
> Under the stars beyond our stars where the reinless meteors
> glow,
> Hotly we stormed Valhalla, a million years ago.

Those lines composed by Kipling on board ship were the nearest either of them would ever come to a description of sex. Life in the bedroom, whatever it consisted of, went unportrayed.

The American writer, Henry Adams, friend of Henry James, happened to be on the SS *Teutonic* at the same time. Kipling put on his scintillating show for him; Carrie remained her undemonstrative self, and Adams drew the usual conclusion: 'In full delight of his endless fun and variety, one felt the old conundrum repeat itself. Somehow, somewhere, Kipling and the American were not one, but two, and could not be glued together.'

The plan was to visit the Balestier estate in Brattleboro, Vermont, and then continue across the world, resuming together the tour which for Rudyard had been interrupted by Wolcott's death. The idea on this first, short visit was to scout out a site for their future home. In the end they spent nearly a month there, and it did not go entirely well. With his wife Mai and their beautiful little daughter Marjorie, Carrie's brother Beatty was ensconced in Maplewood, a farmhouse on the family estate. Beatty intended to receive the newly-wed Kiplings on his own terms. He wasn't going to make any allowances for his elder sister and her smart husband from England. With his sly and subversive wit, he was distrustful of the anglophilia and its cultural snobbery which Kipling and his sister brought with them. Beatty would show them what a real American was like. He was the Brattleboro man, the favourite of their fearsome grandmother Mme Balestier, popular with locals, spendthrift, in debt, and a heavy drinker. He had 'a tongue like a skinning knife. His heart was in twin compartments: lavish kindliness, unbounded hate.' 'No matter what scrap he was in,' one

Vermonter remarked, 'he was real amusin' 'bout it.'

Carrie saw things differently. She, with her world-famous and high-earning husband from England, the hope for the future of world literature, in whose presence smalltime farmers like Beatty should be in awe, would now be the leading Balestier in Brattleboro. If Wolcott had been alive, she would have conceded power to him, but Beatty was inferior, impoverished and unimpressive. All the Balestiers were good haters, and she would put him in his place.

Kipling, for his part, was entranced by the silence and glitter of the Vermont winter. The way the sleighs glided over the frozen roads; the muffled privacy of the snow-thickened woods; the view to the mountains on the skyline: all this sharp clarity was precisely what he had come to America for. And they began by having fun with Beatty, Mai and Marjorie. The two families played together in the snow and dined together in Maplewood.

It could not last. Even on this short visit, within a couple of weeks the hostility latent between Carrie and her brother surfaced. They argued over money. Carrie and Kipling made the mistake of offering to buy Beatty's farm from him. He was already in debt; they were awash with dollars as the royalty payments came flooding in from across the world. Maplewood was a wonderful, warm house, precisely the kind of haven Kipling needed. But for a man such as Beatty, whose dignity was tender, who had already suffered years of condescension from his sister, it was difficult to think of a more crass suggestion. Inevitably, Beatty refused. Instead, he agreed to sell them 11 acres of his land for $750, a price Carrie thought scandalous.

Soon afterwards the Kiplings resumed their honeymoon journey around the world. En route, the bank in which Kipling's money was on deposit collapsed, a catastrophe which forced them to return early from their travels. But that was a minor ripple in the ocean of happiness that seemed to lie before them. When they returned in the midsummer of 1892, Carrie was pregnant and Brattleboro looked more beautiful than England ever could. They rented a little house, called Bliss Cottage, for $120 a year and hired a maid for $18 a month. The royalties and magazine fees poured in. Henry James heard on the transatlantic grapevine that Kipling was 'supremely content... *en puissance de femme*'. Construction began on a large new house perched on the hillside they had bought from Beatty. In an act combining charity and dominance, they hired Beatty as the foreman of the works, through whom the craftsmen and labourers would be paid.

This was the period on which Kipling would look back as the happiest of his life. He was beginning on the stories which would be collected in *The Jungle Book*. But Carrie could scarcely be so content. It soon became clear that to have settled in Brattleboro was a mistake. The convoluted emotional landscape of the Balestier estate was far from peaceful. Carrie's grandmother, old Mme Balestier, with a profile that would not have been out of place on Mount Rushmore, as craggy as a Navajo chief, presided at the big old mansion of Beechwood, indulging Beatty and suspicious of both Carrie and Carrie's mother, Anna. The wider family was equally riven. Carrie's uncles – her father's brothers – were so locked in mutual loathing that they would never visit Beechwood at the same time. The programme of the year had to be meticulously divided up so that no male Balestier was in danger of meeting any other.

Kipling, reading the exterior calm of Vermont, thinking that he had arrived somehow at a northern Arcadia, failed to understand the underlying realities. What he took for a haven was in fact a battleground. Carrie and her brother soon started to argue. As the work progressed on the new house, she became increasingly suspicious of him, thinking he was diverting the money into his own pocket, and treating him with a miserliness which any man would have resented. Every payment, in and out, was meticulously noted in her diary. In November 1892, for example, she received a cheque for \$3,888 from Macmillan and Methuen (sent by Kipling's London agent, AP Watt) and during the course of the month she made payments to Beatty every three or four days: for $2.25 on the 4th, $50 on the 11th, $20 on the 15th, $7 on the 17th, $20 on the 24th, sinking to the low point in this pitiable process of $1.50 on the 28th. Beatty rankled under the humiliation.

The house, initially to be called The Crow's Nest and finally christened Naulakha after the novel on which Kipling had co-operated with Wolcott Balestier, was the first of their fortresses against the world. It was designed to turn its back to the public road – and incidentally to the Beatty Balestiers, who lived just opposite the entrance to its driveway. Naulakha was set as far from the road as it could be. Its windows and doors were placed so that no passers-by could see in. It was only one room deep, with corridors and the only entrance along the uphill side.

The desire for privacy was intense but not mad. Kipling was already subject to the attentions of reporters as he went about his daily business. A conversation in a public carriage was noted down by an undercover reporter and reproduced verbatim in the press. Kipling was one of the first to manipulate, to benefit and to suffer from the modern star-system.

Kipling's study was at the end of the house looking out to the south and east. Here the defences thickened. Bookcases were built across the lower half of the windows and the glazed part above them was filled with Tiffany stained glass. Access to this workroom, the prow of the house as Kipling described it, could only be had through Carrie's own office. There she guarded her husband, and the room, in which she laboured at their accounts and the correspondence with her husband's widespread interests across the world, became known in Brattleboro as 'the Dragon's Lair'. The phrase bears all the hallmarks of Beatty's wit. But it is Kipling's marine analogy which gives the fuller picture. He may have been at the prow of the ship, thrusting out into the landscape, but it was Carrie who was on the bridge, controlling and directing, the buffer between her husband and the world.

The grandeur of the Kiplings and Carrie's affectations was generally despised. He was always slovenly in appearance. She was smart beyond all discretion. 'What makes them build at all,' it was asked in the town, 'when there are plenty of large farms with good enough buildings for anybody to be bought at half the price?' Aloofness is not a route to popularity and its source would probably not have been understood. Both Rudyard and Carrie felt a general distrust of America. Already in London Carrie had written to her sister on the vulgarity and coarseness of American culture, and for Kipling, in some ways entranced by the vigour and openness of American life, the country nevertheless represented a terrifying and dangerous lawlessness. America was anarchy without tradition. 'So far the immense natural wealth of the land holds this ineptitude up... *Au fond* it's barbarism – barbarism plus telephone, electric light, rail and suffrage but all the more terrible for that very reason.' Beatty, in his loose-lipped ease and his disorder, was Americanness itself, the sense of incipient anarchy which both Rudyard and Carrie loathed and distrusted. He represented the great erosive force against which they had to set themselves. And now they were being compelled to live with it in conditions of almost intolerable intimacy. They would do all they could to repress and reject it.

Relations between Carrie and Beatty's wife Mai worsened. Carrie was said to be jealous of her beauty and perhaps alarmed by the relaxed, companionable atmosphere in Maplewood, their farmhouse. It pulsed with the warmth which Bliss Cottage – known as the Blizzard – seemed somehow to lack. Carrie tried to patronise Mai, consoling her on the hopelessness of her husband. Mai would have nothing of it.

For all that, there could be real gaiety at Bliss Cottage and after they moved into Naulakha. At the end of 1892, a daughter was born, named Josephine after her aunt. Kipling skied in his meadows and bought his wife a beautiful red phaeton sleigh. Parties were held in the barn, lit with kerosene lamps, with cider to drink and sandwiches to eat, for which Kipling pinned up notices saying 'Here are the marble pillars!' 'This is the gilded divan!' And as Josephine grew she became astonishingly beautiful.

The National Trust Photographic library

Carrie and Rudyard with Josephine, 1892

Bo, as he called her, always had smiling eyes. She ran barefoot in the garden. Kipling, with his new pocket Kodak, endlessly photographed her – in the snow and the pretty summer meadows, on the tigerskin rugs with her hair arranged around her like a halo. Occasionally, Mme Balestier, her great-grandmother, appears distantly in the photographs, marmoreal, a huge hook nose and drawn-back hair, a prefiguring of Carrie herself. Josephine seemed to have little of that Wolcott-Balestier heaviness. She looks as slight and clever as Kipling's mother, of whom the Viceroy of India had once said, 'dullness could not exist in the same room'. Josephine dances in the photographs along the gravel paths, wheeling her wheelbarrow past the stone walls, while her mother looks on. Carrie has grown fatter now. Her torso and shoulders have become massive, leg-of-mutton sleeves ballooning around them, and her whole manner has become both withdrawn and stolid. The early acquisitiveness has been replaced by something more defensive and less sure. In many of the pictures, she stands unwillingly in front of the camera, substantial in patterned Chinese silk or summer linen. Beside her, Josephine shines, sensitive, imaginative, precocious, 'singing, shouting, bubbling from dawn till dark', as her father described her. She is the most dearly beloved, the most perfect girl.

As his love poured into his daughter, Kipling became neglectful of his wife. He was now applying to her his habitual recourse to absence and retreat. He made frequent sorties from Brattleboro, escaping the control system that Carrie had developed, and moving happily and easily into the urban male world which adored him. He was away visiting friends in Boston, when Naulakha was finally finished, and so contributed nothing to the process of moving in. Carrie, with her young baby in her arms, was left to do it all. 'Carpenters, painters, plumbers and ditch-diggers all about us', she wrote in her diary. 'It is quite the worst day I ever spent in my life. No words can paint my discouragement and utter dreariness.' He visited friends in Boston and Carrie was left behind. On his return he scowled at her, told her that she was mismanaging the household. The atmosphere clearly depressed even the staff. There were repeated crises, which Carrie was forced to confront alone. 'Both maids leave,' Carrie moaned to her diary. 'Cook because waitress does, waitress because she won't wear a cap with lace frills.' It was to be the first of many chain-resignations in the Kipling household over the years to come. Carrie did not, it would seem, have the knack of charming her employees. Left alone, she became the butt of Brattleboro ridicule.

Mai and her friends confessed to each other they thought there was something a little mad about Carrie Kipling. Her grandmother's maid, a fierce Irish Kate, had once slammed and locked the door of Beechwood in Carrie's face. Carrie's attempts at dignity looked absurd. Their imported English servants were ludicrous – a coach-man who was said to have been in the service of an earl, and 'a nurse', it was gossiped 'who applied for the position with the avowed desire to devote her life to the child of a genius'. And as for Naulakha, wasn't it hideous and uncomfortable? She was not, Brattleboro opinion decided, 'a natural housekeeper'; and, in the words of a neighbour, the super-Wasp Molly Cabot, she 'kept the machinery of life always in evidence. An unexpected guest at luncheon would have been an impossibility. Nor did she know how to make a house attractive.' Compared with the lush, late-Victorian manner of most of the grander Brattleboro houses, Naulakha's stripped Arts-and-Crafts aesthetic looked bony in the extreme. 'Meagre furnishings augmented by cotton hangings from India,' was Cabot's verdict.

The husband was scarcely better. By early spring 1896, when the Kiplings' second daughter Elsie was born, he had become extraordinarily touchy again. Approached by reporters on the road, he suddenly erupted into a rage: 'I decline to be interviewed... It is an outrage to be insulted on the public highways and asked to give details of one's private life... Your copyright laws have swindled me out of considerable money. Is it not enough to steal my books without intruding on my private life? When I have any...'

Meanwhile, the bitterness between the Beatty and the Carrie households had become open war. A disagreement erupted over the use of the pasture in front of Naulakha, where Carrie wanted to plant a formal garden. Beatty was accused of stealing milk from the Kiplings' kitchen. Carrie said that Marjorie, Mai and Beatty's daughter, was a bad influence on her own precious Josephine. Then Beatty fell out with Matt Howard, the Kipling's coachman and foreman, driving back and forth across the road one day to prevent him passing. But there were vast reservoirs of pride at stake. It was understood in the village that 'Kipling carried Beatty' – a subliminal choice of word: if anyone, it was Carrie doing the carrying. As a result, Beatty's unpaid accounts in the Brattleboro stores were allowed to run on, his debt ever deepening. The Kiplings by now, of course, had no intention whatsoever of bailing him out.

At last, Carrie accused Beatty of appropriating money which should have gone on the construction of Naulakha. A couple of local firms were pursuing him for unpaid bills. She tried to persuade her mother to withdraw their guarantee for Beatty's mortgage on Maplewood, thus driving him into bankruptcy. It looked to Beatty and Mai as if Carrie was trying to get hold of Maplewood for herself. She had already, with the insensitivity and grandeur which had coloured all her relations with her brother, offered to look after Mai and Marjorie for a year or so while Beatty went off and dried out somewhere else. The family split over the issue. Josephine Balestier, the younger sister, sided with the younger brother, alienated by Carrie's patronising treatment of her over many years.

Anna Balestier refused to play her part in the bankruptcy plan. 'Beatty is a gentleman,' she told her daughter, 'drunk or sober.'

Beatty, of course, even through the distortions and self-deceptions of alcoholism, would have seen the Kiplings rolling in money and been appalled at any idea that they shouldn't do well by him. Beatty was warned of the bankruptcy plot by his sister Josephine and went up to Naulakha to explain where the construction money (all $11,175 of it, as Carrie noted in her diary) had gone. Carrie refused him entrance, so Beatty sent a letter, to which Carrie never replied.

Finally, this long confrontation of mutual prejudice and mutual distrust, of family relationships poisoned by money, came to a climax. Beatty met Kipling on the Brattleboro road, the drunk American in his buggy and the standoffish Englishman just dusting himself down having fallen off his bicycle:

Beatty: See here, I want to speak to you.

Kipling: If you have anything to say, say it to my lawyer. [The apostle of action and manly courage retreating into pomposity and the haven of legal proprieties.]

Beatty [his cheekbones said to be 'blue with passion']: By Jesus, this is no case for the lawyers. I want you to understand that you have got to retract those goddamn lies you have been telling about me. You've got to do it inside a week or I'll kick the goddamn soul out of you.

Kipling: Let us get this straight. Do you mean personal violence?

Beatty: Yes, I'll give you a week and if you don't do it I'll blow out your goddamn brains.

Kipling: You will have only yourself to blame for the consequences.

Beatty then called Kipling 'a liar, a cheat and a coward'. At that moment, by chance, Matt Howard, the coachman, came up and bundled Kipling away. For the rest of the day, he did nothing, unable to work, in despair at this outbreak of violence in his life. He lay incompetent to act. Carrie pressed him and eventually he succumbed. He visited his lawyer. He could do no work. Carrie and he planted seeds together in the garden. Three days later Beatty was arrested. He was charged with 'breaking the peace by making an assault on Rudyard Kipling with force and arms' and of 'assault with opprobriums and indecent epithets and threatening to kill'. 'A very warm day', Carrie wrote in her diary 'and so far the most wretched unhappy day of my life.' Kipling had failed to keep his head when all about were losing theirs.

Beatty got in touch with all the newspapers and 'reporters with Kodaks', as Carrie described them in her diary, arrived from New York, Boston, Springfield, Philadelphia and Washington DC. Beatty regaled them with the most fascinating stories he could find.

A magistrate's hearing was held in the Brattleboro Opera House. Beatty and the lawyers played to the gallery; Kipling was humiliated – he was judged the less 'manly' of the two – and made to look like a stuffed-shirt Englishman. Carrie was horrified and miserable, watching her husband reduced to listless pulp: 'Rud a total wreck. Sleeps all the time. Dull and listless and dreary. These are dark days for us.' And the following day: 'Rud very miserable and I most anxious.'

A new hearing was set for September. But Carrie and Kipling were both aware that they could not stay in America. The Vermont experiment had collapsed. The only prospect that remained open to them was a return to England where Rudyard would inevitably swim back into the shadow of his parents, who disliked and disapproved of Carrie. Her own home had been poisoned. No other beckoned them. Their privacy had been destroyed. Kipling's weakness meant he could do nothing to sustain her. Throughout that spring and summer, he would not even walk on his own acres without a companion to protect him in case of attack.

On the day before the Kiplings left Vermont, pretty, gossipy Molly Cabot went to see them. Carrie was packing. 'She was tearful but he seemed frozen with misery. He said it was the hardest thing he had ever had to do, that he loved Naulakha.' That evening Carrie wrote in her diary: 'At last it's all done and I go to my bed with a heavy heart.' It had been a year 'of calamity and sorrow'. Vermont and Brattleboro became yet another aspect of their lives which Kipling could not discuss, pushed into the dark.

***

They were homeless and rootless. They could neither return to the Balestier world of Brattleboro, nor did Carrie want to live anywhere close to Rudyard's parents at Tisbury near Salisbury. Alice still hated and distrusted her, blaming her and her family for the Vermont debacle. Kipling, in a state of collapse, left the arrangements and choice of their next house to Carrie. She settled on a dark mid-Victorian pile near Torquay. It was called Rock House. Perhaps, like Bliss Cottage, the name meant something to her: another attempt at a secure haven.

Under the pressure of the troubles they carried with them, the roles they were playing within their marriage grew further apart. Kipling was the joyful, game-playing flirt and lover of children, giving slices of ham to babies at picnics, singing at the top of his voice as he cycled down the steep hills around Torquay. She was maintaining order, looking after the children and the house, toiling through its duties and its chores. 'Rud goes out on his wheel while I grind at cutting out for the children,' her diary records. 'They all get an outing but baby and myself. I grind at accounts.' She was soon pregnant again with their third child and this time the pregnancy was difficult. Added to the strain already in their lives, her heaviness wore her down and exhausted her patience.

Kipling soon became bored with any kind of solitary life in Devon. He would spend weeks at a time in London, being fêted by the various worlds with which he flirted: the press, the group of Conservative imperialists for whom he had become laureate, the admirals and generals to whose deepest desires and fears he had given unprecedented voice. His poetry appealed to a breed of Englishman who had previously felt despised or ignored by the liberal and aesthetic establishment. In 1897, Captain Caius Crutchley, Secretary of the Navy League, an imperialist lobby group, wrote to him: 'The general tenor of your writing is so patriotic that I cannot resist the impression that you would be willing to assist the Navy League in the work it has undertaken in endeavouring to arouse the apparently dormant spirit of patriotism in the rank and file of the British people.' That was the world in which Kipling felt comfortable. Beside the global scale of his public work, Carrie felt abandoned in the Torquay house. It seemed to instil 'a gathering blackness of mind and sorrow of the heart' whenever either of them went in the door.

Another bout of desperate house-hunting now began. In Kent, near Lewes in Sussex, in Wiltshire, in Dorset, on the outskirts of Hastings: the Kiplings wandered the south of England looking for a home. For several months they lived in the luxurious nightmare of the Royal Palace Hotel in London. As Kipling wrote to a friend, 'We're houseless gipsies now.'

As an escape from gloom and solitude, Kipling invited his enormous, voluble, over-confident network of relations to lunch and to stay. The cousinry of Burne-Joneses, Macdonalds, Baldwins and Poynters landed themselves on Carrie and she bowed beneath the weight. Worst of all were the visits of the Kipling parents and Rudyard's half-deranged younger sister Trix, who would veer from catatonia to endless babbling and whose husband, Colonel Fleming, was stiff, dour and uncommunicative. 'Weary, dreary work and entire exhaustion follows', Carrie confided as curtly as ever to her diary. 'Dec 22 Trix and Mr and Mrs K for Christmas. I am full of labour and preparations...' A few months later, and yet another visit of the parents. 'I drag myself down to preside, and nearly die of misery before bedtime comes to my relief.' Another Christmas and more days of hell: 'Grub on in vain attempts to cheer or divert Mrs Kipling but only solid gloom rewards us.' After they eventually moved to The Elms, a house in Rottingdean on the south coast, the enclosure by the cousinry became even more intense. Rottingdean was as much of a Kipling enclave as Brattleboro had been a Balestier one. Carrie was now living in the enemy camp. She was almost without intimates.

If her life was a mixture of abandonment, exile and self-pity, Kipling tried in his joshing, too-boyish way to make it seem better with a cheerful remark or two. At the end of her diary for 1898, he writes: 'Here ends the sixth volume in every way the richest of the years to us two personally. All but the seventh year of our married life made good by Carrie. "She shall do him good and not evil all the days of her life." Bless you my dear.' It was a superficial response to the increasingly dire condition in which he was leaving his wife.

Their son John had been born on 17 August 1897 and that winter for the first time, seeking sunshine and warmth and a sense of enlargement which the exhausting petti-ness of England could not provide, they had spent the winter in Cape Town. En route, Carrie was as unhappy and run down as she had ever been: 'I feel dull and ill and realise again', she wrote in her increasingly unpunctuated style, 'how unfit I am, how near a thorough breakdown.' A young passenger on the ship left a devastating appraisal of Carrie in her mid-thirties: 'She may have been pretty before she got fat, but she gobbles her food and is dowdy –

does not even dress the children nicely, and they are dear little things.' Kipling – 'very amusing' to the strangers on-board – was said to speak to his wife 'as in duty bound'.

For all their search for a haven, the Kiplings rarely settled in one place for more than a few months at a time. They were always on the move, always looking for some-where else, some other diversion. In January 1899, the family decided to leave England for New York. Carrie wanted to visit her mother and Kipling to deal with some of the problems that were clustering around the American publication of his work. Alice Kipling was firmly against a midwinter crossing with the children, but Carrie overrode her advice.

On 25 January, they went by train to Liverpool and joined the SS *Majestic*. The cabins they had were perfect and, after calling at Queenstown in southern Ireland, the ship headed out into the North Atlantic. The next day all three children were sick in the atrocious winter weather and by the 29th a near-hurricane was blowing around them. In the icy air of the oceanic winter, Josephine and Elsie both fell ill with colds. By 1 February, Josephine was worse and as they arrived in New York Carrie was already wound up to a high state of anxiety. The baby John had now also succumbed. The doctor was summoned to the Hotel Grenoble on Seventh Avenue in mid-town Manhattan. Anna Balestier came to the hotel, accompanied by Carrie's sister Josephine and her husband, Theodore Dunham, a doctor.

By 4 February, as a snowstorm engulfed New York, the children were suspected of having contracted whooping cough. Holed up, besieged by an unbroken train of callers, Carrie and the children were miserable. The mood did not lift. Josephine worsened. A nurse was engaged to relieve Carrie of the night care and to give her some rest. On the 8th, Dr Conland, a great friend from Vermont, came down to New York to attend the family. As he arrived, Carrie herself fell ill with a high temperature. She spent all next day in bed, dazed with the fever. It raged for another three days and by the time she had recovered, the children had too. At last, ten days after their arrival in New York, it looked as if the crisis was over.

On 20 February the family went for a short walk in Central Park and Kipling lunched at the Century Club. That evening, the first signs of a renewal of the illness emerged. Kipling felt 'dull' and in the night started to burn with a fever. The following morning he was too ill to get up and Dr Dunham was called for. He in turn summoned a specialist, Dr Janeway, who diagnosed 'inflammation in one lung'.

Carrie scarcely slept and remained anxious throughout the following day. Doctors came and went. In her diary that night she wrote what was in effect a love letter to her sickening husband: 'Rud so good and patient – sleeps much – good friends lend helping hands and I feel how every one Rud has ever spoken to has loved him and is glad to help do for him.'

By the next day, 23 February, Kipling was now 'sane and quiet', even able to do some writing. But Josephine had fallen ill again. She had a high temperature and fever in the night. Carrie, drained by the worry of her desperately ill family, had to make one of the most difficult decisions of her life. The doctors 'feared complications in Josephine's condition'. That was code for her being in danger. As she later wrote to her mother-in-law, she felt her hands were 'more than full' with Kipling's own illness and that she 'could not properly attend to Josephine'. In a decision that at this distance is scarcely intelligible, she took her daughter, even in the height of her fever, 21 blocks across Manhattan, to the house of a family friend on the Lower East Side. It was 'a moment', as she wrote in her diary the next morning, 'of conscious agony to stand out from the average'.

Kipling sickened. He became delirious. Paranoid and intensely sexual fantasies rattled out of him. A huntedness hung over his face. As Carrie watched, he was making terrified journeys to Robert Louis Stevenson in Samoa, travelling in submarines and living life underground. He saw the nurses attending to him 'dressed throughout in soubrette style, with short skirts, clock stockings and high heels'. At times, as he writhed, an agonised sobbing for breath lurched from his body.

Carrie commuted between the bedsides of her delirious husband and her scarcely conscious daughter – back and forth, back and forth, looking for anything she might do for the people she loved. Josephine was sliding away. On 5 March Carrie saw her three times, once in the morning, once in the afternoon and at ten o'clock that evening. In the night-time, as Carrie sat and stroked her daughter's forehead, 'she was conscious for a moment and sent her love to "daddy and all".'

Josephine died the next morning, at 6.30. Dr Conland, from Vermont, went with Carrie to bury her in the cemetery at Fresh Pond, Long Island. Carrie made no entry in her diary for over a month. Every year, as the spring came round, 6 March would be silently marked in the Kipling household as the 'saddest day of our lives'.

The depths of her reserves were now called on. Kipling was still delirious, unable to understand the realities of the world around him. His pneumonia had now spread to the other lung. He was struggling for life, too ill to be told the news. Carrie was alone with her grief. Telegrams and letters concerned for Kipling's health swamped the Hotel Grenoble. Frank Doubleday, the publisher, was there to help her, cooking for the patient, dealing with much of the mail and saving Carrie from collapse. One dreadful lonely day followed another, until finally, against the opinion of the doctors, she felt she had to tell her husband what had happened. She was advised to wait at least another day but couldn't, and asked Doubleday to go into Kipling's sickroom and tell him of Josephine's death: 'I took a seat beside him,' Doubleday later wrote, 'and told the story in as few words as I could. He listened in silence till I had finished, then turned his face to the wall.'

Carrie felt that at first Kipling was 'too ill to realise it quite, but now every day he feels it more'. As he emerged from the sickness, he had to confront the death of the child he loved more than any other. Visitors to the recovering man saw his wife beside him 'so splendidly restrained and self-controlled but vibrating with sensitiveness and bodily worn by it'.

It is one of the most astonishing aspects of this despised woman that through the greatest crisis of her life she was maintaining the business correspondence which her role as her husband's agent and manager involved. A New York publisher, Putnam's, was threatening to issue a pirated edition of Kipling's works. Less than a fortnight after her husband's return to consciousness, she was writing, for example, to Augustus Gurlitz, a New York copyright lawyer she had retained:

'...Mr Kipling asks me to say that he quite agrees

that suit should be brought against Putnam and Dutton at once.

'I must say on my own account that Mr Putnam is not more fortunate in expressing himself in a letter through his attorney than through his stenographer and that his threat of publicity is wide of the mark.

'Yours truly Caroline Kipling.'

She added, in response to a suggestion from Gurlitz: 'You may be quite sure we shall do no talking to reporters. I have had a long and active experience in not talking to them and you may also depend upon me never to communicate direct with the Putnams or their representatives. We made a final try for a settlement which was not a success and now it is in your hands. You can reach me if needed on the telephone.'

She also managed to send money to England to pay for the gardener and cleaner in Rottingdean, £2 to a groom and £2 for hay, for a pony called Gill, which the Kiplings had bought for Josephine the previous autumn.

Such heroism came at a price. Photographs taken of the Kiplings at a friend's house in Morristown, New Jersey, early that summer, show each of them, sitting on the grass, as pale and weak as seedlings first exposed to the sunlight. Carrie plays with her hosts' Yorkshire terriers, and the two surviving children cluster around their suddenly aged mother. She is bowed and worn. Her hair has turned grey. Kipling's jacket looks as if it is made for another man.

Carrie, aged 37 in 1899, after the death of Josephine

In June they returned to England and Rottingdean. 'We come quietly to The Elms to take on a sort of ghost life.' Josephine was everywhere they looked. They saw her every time a chair was empty, in every green corner of the garden, every movement in the shadows, a shout outside, in the opening of a door. They went to the Cape for the winter but she haunted them there too. 'I have only scraps of mind left me,' Carrie wrote, 'and so no memory except of these black weeks just passed.' She was 'stone-dumb' with grief.

For a while, anyway, she held herself together. The portrait painted of her that August by Kipling's cousin, Philip Burne-Jones, shows her standing taut and upright. Her lips are pursed and her hand is on her hip like a Renaissance courtier. A key dangles on a cord from her waist, the totem of control, and a book, surely an accounts book or the recording diary, is perched precariously in the crook of her arm. It is an image of self-discipline, of a person closed to the world and the sufferings it can impose. The way the book is balanced is a signal of the fragility, the insecurity of that control, its readiness to break. Only in the eyes, which are somehow wettened in the painting, and distant, does Burne-Jones portray the concealed reality of loss and hopelessness.

The house-hunting continued. They found one they liked near Burwash in the Sussex Weald but it was re-let before they could buy it. Kipling obscured his distress by frantic engagement with the worlds of journalism, the Navy and the imperial agenda, relying more than ever on the advice and wisdom of his parents. Carrie was left to grieve in isolation, scarcely connecting with him even when he was there. As she wrote to a friend, discussing another's recent engagement: 'I would not marry a literary man for worlds, they are always doing too much and one can only give them help by being hopelessly dull, so they may relax their minds and rest themselves in the security of one's stupidity. They really need to do nothing more exciting than catch flies when they are not on the stretch.'

By the middle of 1901, Carrie was ready to break. Her husband was dividing his time between naval exercises in the English Channel, where he was a guest on board a destroyer, and his parents' house at Tisbury. Carrie's diary for July and August records the stages of her breakdown:

July

13 Wires from Rud.

14 Two letters from Rud from Tisbury.

15 Four wires from Rud. He returns to Tisbury which appals me. My nurse comes. A night of agony.

17 Rud goes to see Willoughby Manor [a house he is thinking of buying near Tisbury and so anathema to Carrie]. I sink down leagues in my declining stride to reach my actual physical state when not braced by necessity. An awful ghost to live with.

18 Down and down I go. Rud writes from Tisbury.

19 Still down. Rud in Tisbury.

20 Still down. Rud rejoins his ship and into her this evening.

21 Still more down in body my mind doing a series of acts in

a circus beyond words to depict in its horrors. Rud writes from Sandown Bay at anchor.

22 Dreary enough. Rud at anchor off Brighton.

26 Rud at Shillington. I remain empty at the bottom of my collapse I think.

27 I remain stationary at the bottom depth physically.

31 The children return very pleased to see me as I am to see them.

August

3 Rud goes to Tisbury. I cannot realise it. It has shocked me so.

4 Dreadful night trying to think out the black future.

5 Rud means to stop longer away.

6 A night of mental agony leaves me down in the bottom of the pit and well nigh hopeless for the black future.

7 Rud arrives at 6pm. Great rejoicing.

That final phrase is a sardonic not an authentic note. Rejoicing by the children maybe, but not by her. These diary entries have been seen by Kipling's biographers as the self-pity of a hysteric. Perhaps they are something else: the outpouring of grief from a misunderstood and despised woman, whose husband preferred the company of his own parents to her own, and who, with her most treasured daughter dead, now found her one purpose, to serve the man of genius, unvalued.

***

In the spring of 1902, the Kiplings at last found the refuge that would sustain them. A house which they had seen and wanted two years before came back on the market. Bateman's, a large stone Sussex manor house, its windows peering out from under beetled brows, was their idea of home. It was private and protective, away from the noise of the village of Burwash on the hill above it, embedded in the richly wooded landscape of the Sussex Weald, a sanctuary. It was, as Kipling wrote, 'a real House in which to settle down for keeps'.

It still looks much as they first found it: a grey stone lichened pile, beamed and panelled inside, with an oak staircase the colour of molasses. 'It is a good and peaceable place,' Kipling wrote to an American friend in 1902, 'standing in terraced lawns nigh to a walled garden of old red brick and two fat-headed oasthouses with red brick stomachs, and an aged silver-grey oak dovecot on top.'

Its solidity and quiet, its sense of refuge, its slightly closed air, dark inside, revealing little of itself to the casual passer-by: these were the qualities that appealed to the Kiplings. It had no bathroom, no running water upstairs and no electricity, but that was irrelevant. The Kiplings needed a fortress, or at least a fortified nest. 'Dear Bateman's', Carrie wrote in her diary, 'beautiful, serene.'

The usual pattern emerged at their moving in. Kipling was off, busy in London. Carrie was left to cope with the arrangements and the workmen. It went as badly as usual. It was 'a labour and struggle to put things right'. Everything around her was 'chaos and black night'. The removers she had hired were hopeless. Everyone seemed to be falling over everyone else. 'Fought with workmen and cleaners all day long. A terrible day', she wrote in her diary. Kipling turned up when the work had been done, breezily cheerful as usual when his wife was distressed.

Now and then at Bateman's, Carrie's diary, a sump for her despair, continued to record her tendency to depression. Where Kipling concealed his anger, violence and despair behind jokiness, Carrie allowed hers to emerge more constantly, a dripping dissatisfaction with her fate. She almost never laughed and she could not escape from the person she was: hardworking, angry, a controller, full of a sense of disappointment at what life had given her, armoured with distrust.

That wasn't the whole picture. Largely thanks to Bateman's itself, 'a good and peaceable place' as Kipling had described it, for these few years a halo of happiness hovered above the life they led. The place they had found folded its arms around them. They planted trees to screen the house from the lane. They set about acquiring as much of the surrounding country as they could. The house had come with 33 acres of ground, but in a steady stream of purchases they enlarged the buffer between them and the world. Rye Green Farm and 51 acres in November 1903, another 16 acres at Little Bateman's and Upper and Lower Oxfield the following September, Dudwell mill and farm with extra land from their neighbour in February 1905. 'Paid Scrimgeour £7,126 for Dudwell', Carrie wrote in her diary as the deal was done. 'Far more than we can afford but of so great an importance to the safety of Bateman's we cannot afford not to.'

The safety of Bateman's was indistinguishable from their own. The process went on, through 14 separate conveyances, until 1928 and, by the end, they had assembled about 300 acres, most of the valley in which the house sits. 'Bateman's looking beautiful', Carrie would write in her diary, on returning to it from a raid on the urban or the social. 'The peace of its shelter never more welcome.'

Any figure resembling Carrie rarely appears in Kipling's stories. Henry James had decided that his friend knew 'almost nothing of the complicated soul or of the female form', but there is one story, called 'An Habitation Enforced', first published in 1909, in which his wife is clearly the model. It is a sentimentalised portrait. There is no mention of Carrie's instability or her irritatingly puritan conscience. But the story at least represents his picture of how his marriage might have been, of how he wished it was, a companionship of loving coherence and mutual support against a difficult and erosive world.

An American couple come to England, for the balm and cure of the landscape. The husband has broken down from overwork. They fall in love with a beautiful and slightly dilapidated estate called Friars Pardon (for which you can read the sacred blessings that Bateman's could bestow).

One day the husband announces to his wife the successful conclusion of the deal:

> 'Friars Pardon – Friars Pardon!' Sophie chanted rapturously, her dark grey eyes big with delight. 'All the farms? Gale Anstey, Burnt House, Rocketts, the Home Farm, and Griffons? Sure you've got 'em all?'
>
> 'Sure.' He smiled.
>
> 'And the woods? High Pardons Wood, Lower Pardons, Suttons, Dutton's Shaw, Reuben's Ghyll, Maxey's Ghyll, and both the Oak Hangers? Sure you've got 'em all?'
>
> 'Every last stick...'

Many of those names are adaptations of places within walking distance of Bateman's and this stylised exchange is a litany of possessiveness and protection. For the Kiplings, the ownership of a wide slice of ancient England was a stay against confusion. It was the one constancy in their life. The memory of Josephine continued to haunt them. They were both frequently ill. In her early years at Bateman's Carrie had cysts cut out of her head and a tumour from her back. Kipling suffered recurrences of the partial paralysis which had afflicted him during their engagement.

By now his public reputation had begun to take the plunge from which it has never recovered. Oscar Wilde had called him 'our best authority on the second-rate' and most of the London literary world was now beginning to agree. The public accolades he received, including in 1907 the Nobel Prize, meant little to him. 'I am disgusted to find how little it really touches one. At first I thought it might be my liver, but I think it must be temperament or the horrid effects of early success.' The private landscape of their house and valley provided the only consolation there was.

Later in 'An Habitation Enforced', Sophie learns she is pregnant. For Kipling, whose own childhood had been stolen from him and who continued to mourn the loss of his first-born daughter, this is a highly charged moment. Sophie – the ideal of his wife as she might have been; her name means wisdom, the one quality Carrie could never claim – was allied to the beautiful substance of their house and to the promise of new life in a vision of perfection for which the Kiplings longed but never achieved:

Of a sudden the house she had bought stood up as she had never seen it before, low-fronted, broad-winged, ample, prepared by course of generations for all such things. As it had steadied her when it lay desolate, so now that it had meaning from their months of life within, it soothed and promised good. She went alone and quickly into the hall, and kissed either door-post, whispering 'Be good to me. You know! You have never failed in your duty yet.'

The real Bateman's, with its herds of Guernsey and Sussex cows, the cream and butter from the dairy, their chickens, geese and bees, the over-brimming pots of Bateman's honey, their pigs and Aberdeen terriers, the pony, Stella, for their children, their gardeners, maids, cooks, chauffeurs, secretaries, governesses, their steady income, their enveloping valley, their illusion at least of rootedness, their friends and cousins, arriving in an unbroken stream for lunch or tea or to stay, was, in its way, a kind of oasis, a claim on happiness.

> Scent of smoke in the evening
> Smell of rain in the night,
> The hours, the days and the seasons
> Order their souls aright.

These were their brief moments of well-being: the day Carrie started a stamp collection with her short-sighted son John, when she went with Elsie to milk the cows, when Bateman's glowed for a while in the autumn evenings, dressed in the flawlessness of its oaks and meadows.

**

John Kipling's fate was settled from the start. 'One small craft,' his father had announced to a naval friend within a week of the birth in 1897, 'recently launched from my own works, its weight (approx) 8.957 lbs, its h.p. (indicated) 2.0464 and its fuel consumption unrecorded but fresh supplies needed every 2^1/$_2$ hours. The vessel at present needs at least 15 years for full completion but at the end of that time may be an efficient addition to the Navy, for which service it is intended.'

Throughout John's childhood, in which he usually failed to meet his father's expectations, and was treated to the joshing, bucking-up encouragement that Kipling would also give his wife, his worried parents had his eyesight checked, fearful that he would not pass the rigorous Navy test. In 1910, when he was 13, John's eyes were seen to be getting worse. Glasses were prescribed. Three years later, at his preliminary medical exam, he was found to be too short-sighted (6/36 in both eyes – he could not read the second line of an optician's chart unaided). The Navy would never have him.

Come the war, which Kipling had been predicting for

years, it was inconceivable, either to the boy himself or to his parents, that he should not join up. This, after all, was the son of an imperialist laureate, a man who had been warning the nation of the coming fight for the last two decades. Of course John had to go. And no time was lost. War was declared on 4 August 1914. 'My cold possesses me,' Carrie wrote in her diary and Kipling added, 'Incidentally Armageddon begins. England declared war on Germany.' Within a few days, John, an immature boy, still a week short of his 17th birthday, desperate to please his father, jerkily assertive of his independence from him, applied for a commission. He and Kipling were driven in the family Rolls-Royce from one recruiting office to another, trying to find a regiment that would take him. But even the Army wouldn't have him because of his eyes. Desperate for him not to miss the coming fight, Kipling and his son both talked of his joining the ranks, where the standards were lower.

Kipling then decided to bypass the official channels and ask his old friend Field Marshal Lord Roberts to give John a commission in the Irish Guards despite his eyesight. It was settled within days and the boy was fitted with a uniform. The brutal nature of the war had quickly become apparent. Carrie's imagination became gripped by the stories she was hearing. She described to her mother a 'surgeon with the Red Cross with both hands cut off so he could not help the English' and Belgian girls who had escaped to France and had been 'ravished four times in an hour. It's our turn next unless we can keep them out.' This sense of the besieging hoards had dogged Carrie's life for two decades, whether it had been the reporters or the nosy public or 'those without the Law': all of them represented the anarchic mass of the uncivilised. This fearfulness of the threatening alien, which had fuelled their life at Bateman's, was now poured into the nightmare image of those millions of raping and mutilating Germans hungry for bodies or blood.

For years now the four Kiplings – Carrie and Rud, John and Elsie – had clung together within the gates at Bateman's, protected from the outside world. Kipling had written a limerick for Elsie when she was a teenager:

There was a young person of Bateman's
Who was guarded in most of her statements.
When asked 'Where's your pa?'
She said — 'Out in his car'
Whereas he was really in Bateman's.

Now, though, John was to enter the very cockpit in which these horrors lived. He was to leave the precious enclosure. John joined his regiment and Kipling, as might be expected, collapsed with the strain, one side of his face paralysed. Carrie attended to him much of the night.

'I must get Rud better,' she wrote to her mother, 'and feel sure his illness is the form the strain anxiety and sadness of these last dreadful weeks have taken. He sleeps and sleeps even today now the temp has left him he slept over an hour this morning.' She wheeled him in and out of the house, exposing him to the sunshine whenever it shone.

At Bateman's they set about preparing for the German invasion. All Kipling's manuscripts and many of the household valuables were sent away. 'When the Germans come', Carrie told her mother, 'they will find very little.' Belgian refugees had flooded over the Channel, reliant on English charity. With confirming horror, Carrie described to her mother two Belgian children she saw, aged six and seven, both without hands. She and Elsie began on a labour they would continue for the rest of the war, knitting mittens and socks for the men in the trenches.

In the autumn of 1914, two of Elsie's friends, already out in France, were killed. The Kiplings' own friends began to lose their sons. A man they had met on a series of skiing holidays before the war was reported shot and killed. At Bateman's, a long, damp winter crept up on them. The entire family contracted colds. The gardener Martin had lumbago, the chauffeur Moore a liver chill. The thought of John, drilling with his men in the open, agonised his mother. It was the cold and the wet that troubled her most. 'My John must have spent hours in the open,' she wrote to her mother in November 1914. 'I am always afraid his turn will come while the bad weather and short days last.'

The brutality which lurked as a kind of unacknowledged undercurrent in the Kipling household now found its vicarious outlet. Alongside the horror stories ('Did I tell you the story of the wounded German prisoner', Carrie wrote to her mother one day, 'who had a woman's hand in his pocket with rings on it?'), there was the cold-hearted justification for the Allied strategy and the pouring of men into the pit of Flanders. 'The idea is', she wrote, 'as long as the Germans will bring their men and feed them to us to kill it's a good job to let them go on.'

At Christmas 1914, when Kipling gave Carrie a cheque intended for Belgian refugees, and she gave him one for the wounded Indian soldiers, she fell ill and went to bed, staying there for days. For the first time in their married life there were no presents for Kipling's birthday, on 30 December. For months, the family stood on the lip of the precipice. All of them were ill in turn. Elsie felt that 'soon she [wouldn't] know any man alive'. Kipling's face ached so that he could not sleep. Carrie maintained her programme for making socks and mittens, dragooning as many of her friends, family and acquaintances as she could into the effort.

'First last and all the time I want socks,' she wrote

to her mother, 'a ten-inch leg and 11 in (long) foot – counting the heel. It sounds large but it's the size wanted, and this and hospital wants are continuous – night shirts in flannel and cotton, pyjamas for hospital and day flannel shirts also.'

John was always asking for new pieces of field equipment to make his life on exercise more comfortable. Elsie was usually sent to London to buy them for him. In the meantime, Kipling's own career had to be administered as usual and Bateman's had to be run. 'If one could get rid of one's responsibilities and turn off servants and live in a cottage all the trouble would be over; but one can't turn them adrift and there we are.' Kipling's humour had by now turned to its most rancid. He had heard that the Germans were making margarine out of their soldiers' corpses. Guests to Bateman's tea, spreading butter on their scones, were treated to this:

Charlotte, when she saw what Hermann
Yielded up when he was dead,
Like a well conducted German
Spread him thickly on her bread.

At the same time, he was writing his famous story 'Mary Postgate', in which the heroine, an English nurse, has an orgasm at the sound of a crashed German airman finally dying in a fire which she has lit to burn him:

She leaned on the poker and waited, while an increasing rapture laid hold on her. She ceased to think. She gave herself up to feel. Her long pleasure was broken by a sound that she had waited for in agony several times in her life. She leaned forward and listened, smiling. There could be no mistake. She closed her eyes and drank it in. Then the end came very distinctly in a lull between two rain gusts. Mary Postgate drew her breath short between her teeth and shivered from head to foot. 'That's all right,' said she contentedly, and went up to the house for a luxurious hot bath before tea.

Over the lives of the Kiplings hung the fate of their son. Early in 1915, Rider Haggard, an old friend, met them in London: 'Neither of them looks so well as they did. Their boy John, who is not yet eighteen, is an officer in the Irish Guards and one can see that they are terrified lest he should be sent to the front and killed, as has happened to nearly all the young men they knew.'

Carrie heard that John was too young to be sent to France before early summer. But the news was little consolation. If there was 'an unexpected shortage of officers in his regiment' he would be sent straightaway. In March, some of the older men in the Irish Guards began to be sent out to France. 'As always, we wonder when his levee will come.' By the beginning of May, as the Sussex spring was starting to bring light and greenness again into their lives, Carrie had begun to write of the coming inevitability with clarity and dread:

'I am feeling so tired and ill. No more news about John. The Guards Brigade will be in the next fight and the reserves now at their base Harve [sic] will I suppose be moved up... meantime we wait and everything changes in a day. All hospital accommodations are being enlarged for the great rush which will come after the next big battle. I hate writing about the war but it is on top of me of course.'

Carrie could think of nothing else. A new threat of Zeppelins dropping gas bombs kept her awake at night. Every aspect of the weather became a sign of what was happening across the Channel. When the wind blew from the east, not only did the sound of distant gunfire reach them, but they imagined they could smell on the wind the gas which the Germans had released across the Allied trenches. When the rain fell on Sussex, all it meant was mud in France. The Kiplings offered Bateman's to the War Office as a hospital but the offer was refused. Carrie kept on with sewing her 'hopeless case shirts'. At every opportunity, John was brought home from his barracks at Warley near Brentwood, for nurture and comfort, for good food and rest, for their company, as much for them as for him.

'Little Johnny Kipling', as his fellow officers called him, 17 years old, 5 foot 6½ inches tall, played the blood as far as he could. Kipling, as a loving father, had given him a car, a Singer called 'Car-uso', and John would describe like a Boy Scout his adventures to his parents: 'I went on the "Razlle-Dazlle" last night. Dinner at Princes, Alhambra and Empire next, then supper at the Savoy, then Murays and two other night-clubs of lesser repute. I left Town in the Singer at 10 past 3am and got here at 7 minutes to 4 (43 mins); that is "going some". I only met 2 taxies a cart on the way down being broad daylight I could move like hell.'

There was no razzle-dazzle for Carrie, though, who lived exposed to the dread. 'Sometimes the uncertainty drives me nearly off my head,' she told her mother. 'There seems for a bit no chance of John's going out to France but any day or hour the summons may come and one has to be ready in one's mind to face it.'

In fact, John's regiment was suffering more than they had expected. Eighteen officers were killed or wounded in one fight. John wrote to tell her in early June that he was under orders for the front. That was no resolution. It didn't mean he would go, only that his mother and sister had to prepare yet again the kit as he wanted it. 'I am so uncertain and anxious,' Carrie wrote to her mother. 'One is really harassed day and night now. Dear love from C...'

As the summer dragged on, the Kiplings and all their relations scoured the casualty lists for the dead and wounded from John's battalion. Others of their friends continued to lose their sons. Kipling's beloved Aunt Georgie, a radical who had been opposed to the war, wrote to Carrie in early August:

'My Carrie –

'I cannot write what is at my heart about you – nor would it serve any good for me to try. I send you my tender love.

'I can say no more – and you will know I am loving you all through.'

Eventually, in early August, Carrie wrote to her mother the words which had been hanging over everything she had done and said since the war began: 'You write you don't see where one finds the courage to send a boy but there is nothing else to do. The world must be saved from the German who will worse than kill us all if he is allowed a chance and one can't let one's friends and neighbours sons be killed in order to save us and our son. There is no chance John will survive unless he is so maimed from a wound as to be unfit to fight. We know it and he does. We all know it, but we all must give and do what we can and live on the shadow of a hope that our boy will be the one to escape.'

A week after Carrie wrote those words, John came to

see her at Bateman's and then returned to his barracks. Both mother and child knew that this was the last time they would see each other. 'John off to Warley at noon,' Carrie wrote in her diary. 'Looks very smart and straight and brave and young as he turns at the top of the stairs to say "Send my love to Daddo."' They were almost the words Josephine had used 16 years before.

The following morning, at 3.30, Carrie 'woke with a bang'. It was precisely the moment at which John was to parade his platoon before embarking for France. Kipling himself, sunk in depression, was ill in bed. His health now took a turn for the worse. What the doctors consistently diagnosed as gastritis, and which Kipling secretly feared was cancer, prevented him from sleeping. The pain in his stomach would not leave him for the rest of his life.

John crossed to France on his 18th birthday. Thereafter, news from him was intermittent. The only address they had, as Carrie wrote to her mother, was:

'John Kipling Esq
2 Batt, Irish Guards
Guards Division, BEF
BEF meaning British Expeditionary Force.'

Everyone at Bateman's suffered. Elsie, strained over the loss of so many of her friends and the general sorrow and anxiety, became increasingly difficult. Carrie's handwriting in her letters now became huge and erratic, her pen taking wide uncertain loops, each line moving in unpredictable directions across the page. 'They say they can't get the Germans to go up to our Cavalry now unless they shoot them from the back,' she told her mother. 'But we are only 180,000 strong and they are millions.'

On the other side of the Channel, on the wide flat chalky plain of northern France, the army was preparing for the Battle of Loos. Night after night in September the working parties went out digging. Miles and miles of assembly trenches and communication trenches were dug and the long lines of glistening white chalk, in full view of the Germans, were impossible to miss. In the ten nights before the battle, they dug 12,000 yards of them. The Germans knew that an attack was coming.

Beneath the chalk lay rich seams of coal and the landscape was littered with pithead gantries and their associated sheds and showers, many of which were still working. Johnny Kipling's battle was to be in a coalfield. At Bateman's a harvest moon hung over the wheatfields as the day of battle approached. John wrote to his parents of the heat and dust in France, the long marches, the digging of trenches and a great longing for battle. 'When he is in the trenches proper', Carrie wrote to her mother, 'he will have more rest, though more strain.'

She busied herself with the farm and her provisions for the soldiers. She had been told that more than a million mittens were needed for the coming winter. 'I am very busy as we are taking over some of the farms that up to now have been let, thinking that with more capital than the usual small farmer has we can grow more food. It's a big undertaking but again it must be done as we must grow all the food we can.'

On Monday, 27 September 1915, she had a letter from John written the previous Thursday. 'We have been marching for 48 hours to take up our position. The heat and dust is dreadful so we march at night.' The marches were so long and so hard that he and his men had abandoned most of their equipment. John asked his mother to post him toothbrushes when she could. That Monday the wheat in the Bateman's fields was cut and Carrie was out with her men, urging them to get it stacked and the stacks thatched before the threatening rain fell and spoiled it. By Wednesday Kipling was miserable with gastritis. Elsie and Carrie were continuing to knit a mitten each every day, a pair each on Sundays, 'sending wool and needles in all directions'.

On that Saturday, 2 October, a friend of Elsie's, Isabel Law, daughter of Bonar Law, the Conservative politician, came over to Bateman's to visit her. The two girls walked and talked in the garden and discussed their absent friends. Carrie and Kipling waited until Isabel had left before showing Elsie the telegram they had received that morning from the War Office. John was missing. On Monday, in the late afternoon, he had been wounded and left in a mine building outside Loos. A few minutes later it had been surrounded by Germans.

Carrie was unable to make any entries in her diary for the rest of the month. But on Thursday, 7 October, she wrote to her mother:

'I have no news but the enclosed. Rud and I are agreed that John was not left in the building he went to. I think he would have been taken along with his men and shot with the others. Only one man out of the 200 returned. The telegrams come in hourly from India, Canada, Australia, South Africa. You will like the letter from his Col. It's a nice picture of the gallant boy with his men, leading and encouraging them.

'We do not grudge him for a second. It would have been intolerable to have had him do otherwise than take his part — but the anxiety is almost beyond bearing. One knows how the Germans treat prisoners only too well. We are having warm and delicious weather and I am thankful today Rud is better. He asked me to send his love and say how distressed he was with what you must be feeling.

'Dearest love, C'

Among the letters from his brother officers that she received was one from Captain Bird, Johnny Kipling's company commander:

'Your son behaved with great gallantry and coolness and handled his men splendidly. I trust that your great anxiety may be allayed by definite news of his safety soon.

'Please accept my most heartfelt sympathy. I had a great affection for him.

'Yours sincerely,

'John B Bird'

Perhaps it was a slip of the pen, perhaps a subliminal conveying of the truth, but in using the word 'had' Captain Bird sounded the death-note for John.

The desperate search for news continued for months. The two Kiplings spent week after week interviewing wounded soldiers, searching out anyone who might have seen what happened, writing across the world for any possible source of information obliquely arrived at, hearing one conflicting story after another at wounded bedsides. Two possible versions eventually emerged. He had either been shot in the head while storming a German machine-gun position, or half his face had been blown away by a shell.

For his parents, there was no recovering from this. The fears which both had nurtured for so long, the vision of the world as an encompassing anarchy, had found its resolution here. The death of John was only a confirmation of that world-view, shared by both Kiplings, and which W H Auden later identified: 'Civilisation (and consciousness) is a little citadel of light surrounded by a great darkness full of malignant forces and only maintained through the centuries by everlasting vigilance, will power and self-sacrifice.'

If that is your understanding, then the only route from catastrophe is discipline, courage and repression. That was the life the Kiplings had always followed, and they continued to do so now, a rigid maintenance of order in the face of devastation. It was an effort they were not capable of sustaining unbroken. Their bodies under constant stress began to come apart; the way they treated each other became increasingly harsh and hostile, their dealings with others increasingly filled with rage and contempt.

Later that autumn, Carrie, in response to a letter of condolence, wrote to the owner of the hotel in Switzerland where before the war the Kiplings had often stayed for a skiing holiday:

'We must always keep a window open to hope, since so many officers have turned up after even a year of absence – but as the weeks go by our anxiety – always with us, becomes very heavy. If he met his death fighting for all the things we hold to be of value, we are honoured through him, and though our sorrow is no less, yet we realise he only did what many many Englishmen have done and are prepared to do, and his loss, though so great a thing to us is a little thing to set against the greater.'

That was the public face, the dignified presentation of loss. It concealed a violent and desperate heart. Elsie, the surviving daughter, and the one child for whom neither parent ever had much love, was made by her mother to feel ever more irrelevant, a reminder of what had gone rather than a consolation for it. The world was son-less and so irredeemable.

'25 December 1915 Christmas Day but to us a name only', wrote Carrie in her diary. 'We give no presents and in no way consider the day John not being with us.' Elsie's coming of age in February 1917 also passed almost without celebration. The Kiplings' attention was focused instead on the stream of wounded and shell-shocked officers who, with their families, they were putting up in the Dudwell farmhouse, down the lane from Bateman's: 'Lieutenant Hall and his wife and mother and sister-in-law. Nice folk. Lt Hall a great nerve-wreck from shellshock and gas-poisoning – ill since Sept 28 last, the battle of Loos.' Over the ensuing months, a tragic succession of these officers and their parents, broken sons and grieving sisters, came to stay. Occasionally, they were too much for Carrie. 'Dudwell's guest is rather a bother,' she wrote in September 1917. 'Clings at every turn and is pretty useless.' None was her son.

Carrie's loathing of the Germans became rabid. On

17 August 1917, John's birthday, came 'the news of the Germans big counter-attack at Hill 70 and that they were killed by us in their thousands – So it makes not a bad birthday for our John.' She gave her knowledge of hand-to-hand fighting in the trenches to her mother. 'You may always be sure one Englishman dead means at least five Germans and often ten. With the bayonet it averages seven and it will get worse since the Germans second best must now meet our best.' Obsessively and repetitively, her mind turned to the 'thousands of Belgian refugee girls' who had been made pregnant by German rapists.

The world had closed in around her. There was no lightness here. As for Kipling, his weight had sunk to 8 stone 11 lbs. And his stomach was relentlessly painful. 'There has never been anything like this in all history', he wrote to his friend Rider Haggard, 'the embalming of a race.' Of the 1914-18 British war dead, 472,469 were identified and buried under stones which carried their names. The other 415,325 were never found. Little Johnny Kipling was one of these. The place in which he died was shelled, fought over and churned up three times.

On 13 November 1918, two days after the bells in Burwash church had welcomed the coming of peace, Carrie wrote in her diary: 'Rud and I feel as never before what it means now the war is over to face the world to be remade without a son.' For the rest of their lives, as a form of grieving that continued until the Germans overran Ypres in 1940, the Kiplings paid for a gardener employed by the War Graves Commission to sound the Last Post at the Menin Gate in the city, as a memorial to John.

'Have you news of my boy Jack?'
> *Not this tide.*

'When d'you think that he'll come back?'
> *Not with this wind blowing, and this tide.*

***

For decades Carrie's diaries are thick with complaints about her servants. They were the cause of 'horrid talks'. Their foibles were 'tiresome'. Miss Parker, a secretary who laboured for years in the high-stress Kipling environment, was eventually judged 'a harassing tiresome woman and most incompetent not from lack of ability but with intention'. When she was finally sacked it was, Carrie thought, 'a relief to be done with the strain of it'. Similarly, when Martin the gardener cut his hand on a saw, it was 'utter carelessness. His hand is dressed and as he has cut the tendon will be useless for some time.' When Miss Chamberlain, the replacement for Miss Parker, returned in January 1917 from holiday, it was 'to the distress of all the family who have really enjoyed the rest from her inadequacy'. Within six weeks, Miss Chamberlain had 'become imbecile'. By June she was guilty of 'utter stupidity and muddle' and by the end of the year her employment was over: 'Miss Chamberlain who has been a growing trial because of incapacity and has long been hopeless since her return from holiday declines to work to regulation hours and so will leave my service 5 weeks today. A case of great ingratitude after much forbearance and great tolerance.'

If Carrie was surrounded by frustration, she was never to blame herself. In March 1920, 'Nellie Beeching, sewing maid, who has been taught everything she knows under me, received every kindness for 16 years, comes to say that since her father's death it will be to her advantage to work at home. No word of thanks for all I have done for her. No sign of gratitude. An odd cramped nonconformist woman.' Two days later the Bateman's cook gave notice and two days after that the housemaid.

Carrie could not understand other people. They acted for strange and unintelligible motives. In August 1920, 'The gardener gives notice, no reason assigned, general unrest and fancy and a violent-tempered wife.' In May 1921 Dorothy Ponton, the latest in the line of secretaries, resigned. By the autumn she was back in the Kiplings' employment, but stirring things up in the household. 'September 28 1921: Some of the servants out of sorts from idleness and Miss P not too helpful being too busy being in the right.' This sad catalogue ran on year by year.

When in London with Kipling in March 1923, Carrie calmly recorded in her diary: 'News comes that Cook at Bateman's has a heart attack as well as a sprained foot so we postpone our return.' Later, news of the birth of a son to the chauffeur's wife at Bateman's reached the Kiplings when they were in the south of France. Carrie hoped that now 'all will go well as it's inconvenient to have no chauffeur over here'. It was an attitude that both stemmed from and deepened her loneliness.

Kipling himself retreated ever more deeply into his own privacy. The world could not be trusted and so he would deprive it of what he could. He took to burning the written evidence of his own life. As his sister Trix, in a moment of lucidity, told Lord Birkenhead, one of Kipling's first biographers, in the 1940s: 'If Rud had been a criminal, he could not have been fonder of destroying any family papers that came his way.' One summer, when visiting Bateman's, the American publisher Frank Doubleday, an old friend who had stood by them as Josephine died, and who was known to Kipling by the old Turkish title of 'Effendi', a pun on his initials, discovered Kipling at the grim task. It was a warm summer afternoon, Doubleday was walking down to the house from the station and was amazed to see a thick black plume of smoke emerging from the chimneys. In the tiled hall he found the cause. Kipling was bending down in front of the fire, feeding the flames with masses of paper. Doubleday saw a thick wad of Kipling's manuscripts in that well-known small handwriting disappear into the fire.

'For Heaven's sake, Rud,' he said, 'what are you doing?'

Kipling, perspiring by the blaze, gave the mass of burning papers a rummaging thrust with a poker. He looked up keenly from under those heavy brows.

'Well, Effendi, I was looking over old papers and I got thinking. No one's going to make a monkey out of me after I die.'

Kipling also withdrew even further from his wife. He was either away in London, with the freemasons or his service friends, or shut up at Bateman's with the coterie of Conservative politicians and journalists who looked to him as a mage. Or, more damagingly, he was absent in spirit, withdrawn into the recesses of his own increasingly psychic and arcane writing, or bound up in the privacy of his grief, obsessively and meticulously documenting the history of the Irish Guards in the Great War, as a memorial and testament to his son. Carrie played no part in this life. She was of no interest to his visitors. She was an adjunct, an obstacle to be negotiated en route to him. Nor were their concerns of any interest to her. She ceased to be able to talk – or so Kipling's male friends said – about anything but 'the servant problem'. Her body had turned loose and heavy, her jowls dropped, her hair was no longer kept in the order it always had been. Wisps of it floated waywardly under the brim of a hat, more helmet than hat, beneath which her eyes were unseen. Her breasts were allowed to slump down her chest, a lumpen landslip carried in front of her.

Excluded from everything that mattered to Kipling, Carrie hung on to the externals ever more tightly. Her husband's illness made him an easy victim. Every day from 1919 onwards he was taking pills to relieve what was thought to be the adhesion of his liver to his colon. His eyes were hurting him. He would not trouble himself to argue with his wife. Their separation was invisible. The more he seemed to allow her to control him, the more absent he became. He would pause in the middle of a story to say to her, 'You finish it, Carrie, you tell them how it ends,' which she then would, as one visitor described it, 'with little sniffs'. If he made a mistake, he mutely accepted her correction.

Carrie was left in control of a vacuum. Her loneliness closed in. In 1919 her mother had died. 'Her death', Carrie wrote in her diary, 'tears up all the roots I have left of my child home and life.' Carrie had no contact, beyond an occasional formality, with her younger sister Josephine and none whatsoever with her brother Beatty. In November that year, a fellow officer of John, Captain George Bambridge, came to dinner. He was a huge, fat, sybaritic and stupid man with whom Elsie fell in love. His chin was higher than the crown of Kipling's hat and he liked to have a pheasant feather stuck in the band of his own, like a stage Tyrolese. His paunch bulged both above and below the waistband of his trousers. In May 1924 Elsie told her parents that she wanted to marry him. 'We don't like the idea of loosing her', Carrie wrote in her diary, with a telling slip of the pen, 'and I am appalled at the change it will make.' The Battle of Loos had taken one child. Now the last was to go. After the October wedding, 'We sadly return to face an empty side to our life and for the present are too weary to meet it.' That was her view of existence. She wasn't now actively engaged with life. All she could do was go forward into something that came at her like a flood.

For Elsie, George Bambridge was an escape from a hostile home. 'The two great sorrows of their lives', she wrote after they had died, 'my parents bore bravely and silently, perhaps too silently for their own good.' Too silently, by implication, for hers. Certainly, she had been in love with her father. 'Deftness and certainty of movement were characteristics of his,' she wrote after his death, 'the way he handled things, lit a cigarette. Every gesture or movement was compact of neatness and energy. He never fumbled, and his gestures were always expressive.' But that slight, aerial figure was, she felt, a victim of the domestic atmosphere created by Carrie:

'My mother introduced into everything she did, and even permeated the life of her family with, a sense of strain and worry amounting sometimes to hysteria. Her possessive and rather jealous nature, both with regard to my father and to us children, made our lives very difficult, while her uncertain moods kept us apprehensively on the alert for possible storms.'

Elsie could not see that her mother was the burden-carrier for them all. Carrie shouldered the griefs from which the others hid. She saw her role, even at this tail-end of her life, as the protector and the sustainer. It was her tragedy that the difference between protection and control eluded her. When Kipling was particularly ill, as increasingly he was with a duodenal ulcer that was not diagnosed until 1933, looking old, yellow and shrunken, she hid her anxiety from him. She wouldn't burden him with the idea that she was no longer strong. But, in counterbalance, she could allow him no freedom. When Kipling went out for a walk on his own in the evening, she would be there standing outside the gate on his return to shepherd him back in. She would not let him write to any friend without knowing who the correspondent was. Kipling on occasions had to walk secretly to the village to post his own letters. Once, he gave a single book-end to his friend and doctor, the surgeon Sir John Bland-Sutton, imploring him 'not to tell Carrie'. Of course she knew. When Kipling died, she sent the other half of the pair through the post with a brief note. 'As you've got one, you better have both,' it said.

Eventually, nothing he wrote in his own hand was allowed to leave the house. In 1922, as Kipling reached the end of his vast and wearying work on the Irish Guards, the copy was ready to be sent to the publisher. Kipling had made one or two minor adjustments to the text in pen. Carrie caught sight of the ink-marks on the typewritten pages. 'But this is not the final copy, Rud,' she said, as the long-suffering secretary, Dorothy Ponton, reported it.

'Mr K raised his eyes to Heaven in despair and then glanced quickly at me.

"It's all right, Carrie, I've made only a few alterations, they're quite clear."'

The work was handed back to Miss Ponton to be retyped.

Carrie continued relentlessly to bully the staff. If the secretary was away, she would distribute the wages to them on a Saturday. Usually the process would take five minutes but with Carrie it was a form of ritual humiliation. She would open all the wage packets and query the overtime on every one. In working hours she would supervise them like a matron. Ernest Brown, known as Scout Brown because he was a member of the Burwash pack, who went to work at Bateman's as a houseboy and gardener in 1924, remembered her stalking along the paths. He was weeding a herbaceous border when she came up to him.

' "Scout Brown, how would you like a drive in the car to Tunbridge Wells?"

"Very much, Ma'am," the boy said.

"Well, I'm thinking of taking you to get your eyes tested. Look at the weeds you've missed." '

At Bateman's, 1930s

Somehow the Kiplings still managed to conceal the reality of their lives from the outside world. The Visitors' Book at

Bateman's records hundreds of people coming to see them every year. They could still put on a show when the occasion demanded, especially to the young and impressionable. Courteously, Kipling would greet and entertain them, Carrie making all the necessary arrangements. The novelist Hugh Walpole met them at a party in the early 1930s. He found Kipling: 'Kindly, genial, ready apparently to be friends with anyone but keeping all the time his own guard... Hates opening up reserves. Ma Kipling is a good strong-minded woman who has played watchdog to him for so long that she knows now just how to save him any kind of disturbance mental, physical or spiritual. That's *her* job and she does it superbly...

'He walks about the garden, his eyebrows all that are really visible of him. His body is nothing but his eyes, terrific, lambent, kindly, gentle and exceedingly proud. Good to us all and we are all shadows to him. "Carrie", he says, turning to Mrs K, and at once you see that she is the only real person to him – so she takes him, wraps him up in her bosom and conveys him back to their uncomfortable, hard-chaired home. He is quite content.'

That was scarcely the whole truth. 'A train has to stop at some station or other,' Kipling wrote to a friend. 'I only wish it wasn't such an ugly and lonesome place.' And in her diary Carrie echoed his words. 'I am so wretchedly ill that I can neither read, write or talk and all these days and many more besides I have existed, not lived. There has to be a smash some day.'

After Elsie left, Bateman's became an increasingly lonesome place, vast and gloomy. Illness and dysfunction clung to the house like a sulphur cloud. Kipling on his walks would never greet anyone he met. One autumn he destroyed with his walking-stick the basket of a village woman who was out in his fields collecting mushrooms. Carrie would on occasion threaten Kipling with hints of suicide or self-mutilation, which terrified and cowed him. But then her body started to do it for her. Her doctors told her that she had 'a tired heart'. Cataracts began to appear in both eyes. She had become both rheumatic and diabetic.

The final entry in the Visitors' Book at Bateman's was made on 4-6 January 1936, three days before Kipling signed his will. Twelve days later his gastric ulcer haemorrhaged in London, in Brown's Hotel, and he died of peritonitis. After the words 'Mr and Mrs Mike Mason', entered for those dates, Carrie wrote 'THE END' and underlined it. She never made another entry in her diary, which she had begun on the day she was married.

Carrie hung on for another three years, berating her nurses, who dreaded having to look after her, and destroying with Elsie's help enormous quantities of the Kipling papers. Bateman's was left to the National Trust. Elsie continued to live with her fat husband in an enormous

Georgian pile in Cambridgeshire, where, it was said in Burwash, the footmen wore powdered wigs and rode about on the side of Rolls-Royces. In 1939 Carrie Kipling died, mourned by no one.

ACKNOWLEDGEMENTS

I would like to thank AP Watt Ltd on behalf of The National Trust for Places of Historic Interest or Natural Beauty for permission to quote from the diary and letters of Caroline Kipling, from the letters and work of Rudyard Kipling, and to reproduce the photographs in this book; and Wolcott B Dunham, Jr, for permission to quote from the Kipling-Balestier-Dunham letters. My heartfelt thanks to Bet Inglis and Dorothy Sheridan for their care and helpfulness in guiding me through the Kipling Papers at Sussex University.

SELECT BIBLIOGRAPHY

Kingsley Amis: *Rudyard Kipling* (Thames & Hudson, 1975)

Lord Birkenhead: *Rudyard Kipling* (Hutchinson, 1978)

Molly Cabot: *The Vermont Period: Rudyard Kipling in Vermont* (English Literature in Transition, 1986)

Charles Carrington: *Rudyard Kipling – His Life and Work* (Macmillan, 1955)

Trix Fleming: 'Some Childhood Memories of Rudyard Kipling', *Chambers's Journal* (March 1939)

Ian Hamilton: *Keepers of the Flame* (Hutchinson, 1992)

Amy Hanmer-Croughton: 'The wife of Rudyard Kipling – Caroline Balestier', *Rochester Historical Society Publication Fund Series*, Vol VI (1927)

Edmonia Hill: 'The Young Kipling', *Atlantic Monthly* (April 1936)

Tonie and Valmai Holt: *My Boy Jack? The Search for Kipling's*

Only Son (Leo Cooper, 1998)

Gordon Ireland: *The Balestiers of Beechwood* (privately printed, 1948)

Andrew Lycett: *Rudyard Kipling* (Weidenfeld & Nicolson, 1999)

Philip Mason: *Kipling: The Glass, the Shadow and the Fire* (Jonathan Cape, 1975)

Harold Orel: *A Kipling Chronology* (Macmillan, 1990)

Dorothy Ponton, *Rudyard Kipling at Home and at Work* (privately printed, 1953)

Harry Ricketts: *The Unforgiving Minute – A Life of Rudyard Kipling* (Chatto & Windus, 1999)

Martin Seymour-Smith: *Rudyard Kipling* (Queen Anne Press, 1989)

Frederic F. Van de Water: *Rudyard Kipling's Vermont Feud* (Academy Books, Vermont, 1981)

Angus Wilson: *The Strange Ride of Rudyard Kipling* (Secker & Warburg, 1977)

Adam Nicolson's latest book is Regeneration *(1999) the story of the building of the dome; his many other books include* Restoration *(1998), an account of the rebuilding of Windsor Castle following the fire; and* Perch Hill, *a collection of his columns on rural life written for the* Sunday Telegraph. *He is 43 and lives in East Sussex with his wife and children.*